Silent Music

What would happen if you tried to sing

And no words came out?

Silent Music

Joelle Hope Warden

ACKNOWLEDGEMENTS

Hi! My name is Joelle. I am ten years old and this past summer I wrote my third book.

Like my other books, any money I make from the selling of this book is going to Feed My Starving Children and my college fund. Feed My Starving Children is an organization that sends food to children in need. My college fund is there because I may not become a writer, but I definitely want to go to college.

The idea for this story was inspired by other books such as Wonder and Mockingbird , but creating it helped me I give special thanks to my dad for all his help this year walking with me as I developed the story and sending it to the publisher, to my mom for helping with the cover design and placing the pictures into the story, and my language arts teacher Mrs. Nolan for helping revise my writing and coaching me.

Hope you enjoy this book and make inferences to your own life.

Starting at the End

We finally arrived at the Juilliard School of Music where I had dreamed of going since for as long as I could remember. After tryouts and campus tours and countless applications, I made it! Mom and Dad helped me register at the Welcome table, and I got keys for the dorm and my own room. Wow, my own room.

We gathered up all my luggage and went up the stairs. Dad carried most of my stuff.

“Dad, I can take some of that.” Mom said with a look of concern.

“No, dear. I got it.” Dad grunted with a mixture of pride and strain.

When we got to my room, my roommate was already there. The room was plain white brick with one bunk bed. There was a desk area for each of us. One bunk already was covered with posters of famous actors.

“Hi. I’m Adabelle.” she said with a chirpy voice. I think she was part sparrow, small, chirpy, and excited. “Can I help you with those?”

“No. No. I got them.” Dad was sweating up a storm.

Adabelle had long silky brown hair and jade colored eyes. She told us she was at Juilliard majoring in drama. My parents talked to her and she understood my condition and the use of my Electro-larynx. I even had her try it out herself. "Holy smokes that was totally sick!" She exclaimed. She got a kick out of that. Right there and then Adabelle and I hit it off ; we started our college road together as best friends.

With tears in their eyes, Mom and Dad left with big hugs and kisses. I shed my share of tears as well. After they were gone, Adabelle and I told one another our stories. She told me of places she had been and how her family traveled all over the world. I told her my story through the use of my electro-larynx.

It was a long night of looking back and recounting the highs and lows of not having my voice and eventually finding it.

Lost

When I was four, I would go shopping with my mom when my dad was at work. I would jump up and down pulling my mom out of the house. Mom had to get some new sheets for Aiden, my little brother. "Hurry up, Mom!" So we went to the Target in the mall near our house. For a four year old, Target was like a big jungle to explore. I couldn't wait.

As we got there, we started walking to the linen area. Oh, so many different things I wanted to touch and see what they were for. A Giant stuffed bear, a super bouncer ball, the newest Polly Pocket, and most amazingly a cool art kit with 64 different color pencils, 12 oil pastels, and watercolors of every shade I could think of. While I was checking it out my mom went to the clothing aisle, not knowing she left me behind. Nor did I notice her leaving me. I was entranced by this art kit. I finally took my eyes off it to tell my mom I wanted it so badly and suddenly I realized that she was not with me. I was very scared because I couldn't call out to her. I couldn't make crying noises, and I couldn't tell anyone I was lost. So I sat and held in the burst of screaming that I longed to let out.

While tears rolled down my cheeks, a worker came over and asked what was wrong. I could not answer her. She tried to assure me that I could trust her and tell her what was wrong. But I couldn't way a word. I never could. She figured out soon enough that I was lost. She took me to the service desk and on the speakers in the mall I heard "A lost young girl. Come to the front desk if you have lost your child." Less than a minute passed and I saw my mom running towards me with baby Aiden in the stroller laughing and loving the thrill of the speed. She wrapped her arms around me and thanked the worker. My mom told me I was a brave little girl and she said I deserved a treat so we went back and got the art kit where all this trouble began.

Six years later I still remembered feeling the frustration inside myself that day, not being able to tell that worker I was lost and how scared I was. If I could only have cried out to my mom the moment I realized she was missing. If I only had a voice like everyone else, things would be okay. I would be normal, but that day I clearly felt I was not. I have felt that way again and again, especially every time I hear someone sing.

Day 1

“Mom, I can’t do this.” I signed, in the car as we were on the way to my first day at school. Up until now I had been homeschooled because my parents thought it would be better for me. Mom was a great teacher of reading, math, and writing, but especially music. Dad was my science and physical education teacher. Science, that was his thing. I loved it. So why start public school now? I was not ready! They thought otherwise.

“Honey, you can do this. It will be fine.” She was trying to be reassuring.

I grasped my mom's hand as we walked in. A younger looking teacher waved and approached us. She was my "special needs" helper. Ugh. Hate being labeled "special needs". Who would like that on their title? Yeah, put it on a t-shirt and I will wear it around the hallways.

"My name is Ms. Kris. I am here to help." Well she seemed nice enough. My mom and her said a few words and then my mom turned to me, kissed me and said goodbye. I got a little red faced. Ms. Kris wrote down a 3-digit number and gave me a school map, pointing out where my locker was. "I need to see another family but if you need anything, please stop by my office anytime. Even just to talk."

I walked down the hallway and looked for locker 152. I was both a bit lost and nervous, even with the map provided. A classmate walked toward me, hopefully a friendly one.

"The name is Brina. What's yours?" she asked. I was too nervous even try to respond. "What? Cat has got your tongue?" She was getting impatient. "What's your problem? Oh, whatever!" and she stormed off. I was upset at my failure of making a new friend.

Everyone was unpacking by their lockers except for me. I was frozen like a deer caught in the headlights as my dad might say. I don't think I even know what that means. A hall monitor walked up to me. I was hoping she would be sympathetic.

"You need to be unpacked by now. Get a move on." So much for sympathy. I wanted to tell her I was lost. It made me think of when I was lost at the mall when I was little. Suddenly Ms. Kris rushed up to the hall monitor and spoke to her and led me to my locker.

"Sorry for being so harsh." said the hall monitor. That was nice to hear.

Boy, was I relieved that Ms. Kris came to my rescue. She's ok. I signed "thank you" to her and started putting things in my locker. I collected my supplies and books for math. Ms. Kris came with me to translate my sign language to my Algebra 1 teacher, Mr. Kendrick, and to the other students. Well, sure I couldn't speak, but I zoomed through that pretest. Mr. Kendrick said that if I kept it up they might move me up to the enrichment program next quarter.

The rest of the day went smoothly except for running into that Brina girl at lunch and seeing her talk to other girls, looking back at me and all of them laughing. I mostly kept to myself that day.

Communication

The next morning I packed my backpack and started to the garage to get my bike. Dad was on his way out as well. He teaches science at the high school level of our school. That means I may have him in a couple years. He caught up to me and handed me a neon pad of stickies and a set of colored gel pens.

“You will know what to do with them when you get settled at school.”

“Uh, thanks dad?" Riding away, I shrugged and waved goodbye. When I got to school I went straight to my locker and unpacked my stuff, got my books and walked down the hallway to Mrs. Hollis's class for homeroom. I sat at my desk and started my morning work spelling sheets. From the corner of my eye I saw Ms. Kris slip in.

Mrs. Hollis started the class saying, "Good morning, everyone."

"Good morning, Mrs. Hollis," all the kids said in unison. This I don't get to hear in home-school. It made me smile.

"This morning we are going to pair off and have a chance to get to know one another better." Sound like a good idea. I listened for my name to spoken. "Will and Sebastian, Zona and Faith, Issac and Joss, Kelsey and Yumiko."

Yumiko. I sat up straighter. Yumiko came up to me and cheerfully said, "Hi. I'm Yumiko. You must be Kelsey." I was nervous and didn't know what to do at first. Then I remembered my stickies. I pulled them out of my pencil case and wrote, "Yes. I'm Kelsey. Nice to meet you." Nothing too creative, but it would do. She smiled at me and pulled out her pen and wrote back, "Let's get going if you want to see the rest of the school. I will show you."

"Great." I wrote back. This was going to work. Yumiko led me out of the classroom and showed me around and I got to see the announcement board. It was overburdened with papers. The I saw the trophy case with many awards. Yumiko mentioned she was on the volleyball team and asked if I might join. I said maybe. We were in science together and were lab partners.

This day was much better than the first. After the day was over, I looked in my backpack and saw piles of used stickies. I think I am going to continue to stuff them in my backpack and look at them at the end of the day. Oh boy. I have to tell dad all about this. And tell Luvie, too.

Luvie talk

I grabbed some carrots and hummus for a snack. I went upstairs and took down Luvie from her place on the highest shelf. We decided that would be the best place so my brother couldn't reach him. You might be asking, "Who is Luvie?" Let me introduce you to him. Luvie is my stuffed Alpaca my parents brought back from their trip to Europe. He is all white. Aiden has a camel colored one. Luvie is my confidant. I talk to him about everything. In my imagination we have this magical spot where we talk and have our snack.

"Hi, Luvie."

"Hello, Kelsey," he snorts with that animal accent of his. All imaginary animal friends have that accent.

"Should I tell Dad about my stickie problem?" I ask him.

"Why not? You really should." Luvies answers were always short and to the point. I like that about him.

"Thanks, Luvie! Now I gotta get to my endless amount of homework."

"Wait, Kelsey."

"Yes?"

"Why am I always on the top shelf in the daytime?"

"Skydiving with Aiden and Fuzzie, I believe."

"Oh yeah." Luvie replies. "I forgot. Love skydiving."

"I Love you, Luvie."

"I love you too, Kelsey."

I opened my life science book. I have a simple four paragraph essay to write on the anatomy of a plant. Dad would know how to do this type of stuff. We worked on these kind of things when I was homeschooled. So I waited until he got home.

After I got the rest of my homework done I heard the door open. Dad was home. I ran down the stairs and gave him a big hug. With my sweetest look, I asked him for help on my science homework. As we sat down and put our heads together, the essay was done easy peasy. Actually he just sat there and cheered me on. I wrote it all by myself but I love his company.

Once done I drew a picture of a pile of stickies and crossed it out. Then I drew a white board with a question mark above it. Dad took a bit of time recognizing what I was drawing. I could have written the words out, but this is our little game of charades we like to play.

“That’s a great idea Kelsey! We will get one right away.” Though I loved looking at the stickies at the end of the day, it was getting too messy in my backpack. I needed something cleaner. So after dinner, Aiden and I walked to the corner store with dad to pick up some groceries, and lo and behold, there was a cute little mini-whiteboard with a dry erase marker and an eraser attached at the end of it. Only five dollars! So I bought it with my own money and couldn’t wait to use it at school the next day.

So True

At lunch I was surrounded by my new so-called friends playing around with my whiteboard. I was so excited to get the attention. Even Brina's friends were sitting with me. We were having so much fun drawing pictures and writing words. Brina just rolled her eyes. Let's fast forward to 24 hours later.

Everyone is sitting with Brina doodling on her magnetic whiteboard in her lunch box. It had an assortment of rainbow color markers. She had to have paid more than five dollars for that one. Only Yumiko remained with me.

"You're not going to sit over there where the cool whiteboard is?" I jotted down on my whiteboard.

Yumiko wrote back, “Nope. Brina is bossy and sorta stuck up.” Then she erased it as soon as I was done reading it not wanting anyone to see it. I am so glad for Yumiko. I was so glad not to have anymore lunches for one. She was a friend that always made it lunch for two.

Something New

It's Saturday! That means a break from school, putting stickers on Dad's graded tests and making homemade pizza with mom. In the afternoon I'll be playing frisbee with Gavin, my Vizsla-Lab mix, for short, Gav my dog. As I promised Aiden, we will make origami parachutes and drop Luvie and Fuzzie off the second floor porch and onto the backyard trampoline and race to be the first to get them. At dinner the topic will be church.

"Church!" Aiden moans. "Service is the most booooring thing eeeeever." He is always the drama king.

“I never look forward to it anymore. We just go there because grandma and grandpa goes there.”

“Don’t be so critical Aiden.” This is mom’s approach. “It’s not the end of the world if we go to church this week. The neighbors have two kids, Danika and Gavril, and they tell us their kids enjoy the local church. It’s very popular, I hear.”

“Popular for the boooring people I bet.” Aiden groans again.

My approach, I thought, was short and sweet. “As long as there’s other girls and a Sunday school program where we are dismissed from the adult service, then let’s go there.” I wrote to show my opinion.

Dad’s approach, “The pizza’s really great, dear!” Yes, he is an avoider.

“Oh…um...about church. I go along with Kelsey. Can we finish eating so the pizza doesn’t get cold?”

Dad was much more interested in eating pizza than talking about church.

Techie

It’s Monday. Ugh. I want to pull the covers over my head and hold off as long as I can. But I am a punctual girl that also doesn’t like walking in late anywhere. Too embarrassing. When I got to school I caught up with Yumiko down the hall.

“What class are we heading off to next?” I wrote on my whiteboard knowing that our schedules matched.

“Technology.”

“Yes!” I thought to myself. I text on my phone all the time when everyone else talks on theirs.

This was the first class of the week. It was a good way to start. Mrs. Kently was very nice, always trying to make the class fun.

“Good morning class.” she said with a bounce in her voice. “Today we’ll start with a game. Open the typing program and open the link I wrote down on the board. We will see who can type the fastest and see what we remember from 6th grade.”

In tech I sat next to Tyler. He’s in a few other classes with me. I gave him the look that said “you’re going down.” He saw me and whispered, “you don’t stand a chance.” We both smiled and got ready.

“Go!” Mrs Kently said and we were off. As we started Tyler noticed my fingers flying across the keyboard. He was frozen...hypnotized by my speed. Took him three seconds to snap out of it and get going himself. Too late though. It took me a minute to finish that race. I bet you it had to be a school record.

I stood up and looked around. Everyone had stopped typing and was staring at me.

“Great job Kelsey!” Mrs. Kentley shouted. “Please take a prize from the basket.”

There were pencils, erasers, candy, toy bracelets and mini dry erase markers. I saw Brina whispering something to Marissa about me being a showoff. I just looked down at my feet, took my prize and sat back down next to Tyler. He looked at me. He could tell right away that I was upset.

"You sure got me Kelsey," trying to cheer me up. I looked up at him and smiled.

"Thanks Tyler." I wrote.

"Don't worry about Bri. She does that all the time."

"I think she likes you Tyler. Always giggling when you are around." I put a smiley face at the end of that note.

"Ewww!" is all Tyler could say back.

I wish I could giggle sometimes. But all I could do is smile a bit more. I guess there are some good people in this school.

Tryouts

I almost feel the water swelling in my eyes. I don't want it to burst out.

Music is after lunch today. Yumiko ensures me that I'll be okay. She sits with me in the back row of the classroom. As class begins, Ms. Finch introduces herself and asks everyone else to introduce themselves. The class goes around, each student states their name. When Yumiko finishes Brina stands up and raises her hand. I am confused. Brina already took her turn.

"Yes Brina." Ms. Finch called.

"I would like to tell you that Kelsey cannot participate." she said smugly.

I got a little red faced.

"I am well aware of that Miss Rosas." Ms. Finch said to Brina. "You will please leave the classroom now and think about being more respectful."

Everyone including me stared at Brina as she and her smart mouth shuffled out into the hall. Ms. Finch continued with class and talked to us about about the variety show. As we worked on our music theory work Ms Finch went out to the hall. She came back in a few minutes. Brina did not.

After class some people stayed to try out for the variety show. I didn't stay. What could I do? The next day the drama teacher, Mr. Stone walked into the music room and announced the results of the variety show try outs were posted on the bulletin board. Right after study hall I rushed to the board to see if Yumiko's name was posted. I looked and looked but didn't see it. What I did see was Kani and her small group of friends jumping up and down like Kangaroos. I also saw something else that caught my eyes and right there and then I had an amazing idea.

The idea

The result covered almost everything else on the bulletin board. I pushed them aside and there were lists to sign up for extracurricular activities such as cheer team, art club, marching band, student council, gardening committee. All fine and good. I was looking for something else. My amazing idea was to try out for orchestra. Now where is the post about that. Oh here it is.

A girl from Kani's group turned toward me. She had a face like Yumiko but a little more rounder. She was Chinese and had long spiky hair. She smiled at me when she saw the orchestra flyer in my hand. She walked over to me.

"Hi, my name is Lin." A soft and warm voice I heard.

Of course I didn't say a word. I couldn't. But I waved and smiled.

"I heard of you and that you are mute."

She did. From whom? Okay that was awkward.

"It's ok. I'll keep on talking. OK?" She seemed nervous, like she didn't know if she seemed nice or not.

I nodded. As she continued introducing herself and chatting about school, I noticed Lin had a viola case on her back. I tapped Lin on the shoulder and pointed at her Viola and then the orchestra flyer.

"You bet ya!" Lin replied to my pointing. "I think you should definitely try out, too."

Kani and her friends were getting ready to go and signaled to Lin. Heading to the bus stop racing to catch up with her friends, Lin smiled and waved goodbye. Lin seemed like a nice girl, and I completely understood her actions. For someone who never tried to communicate to someone who couldn't talk back, she did fantastic. Nervous but good.

I texted mom a picture of the flyer. She texted back, "Great! (:"

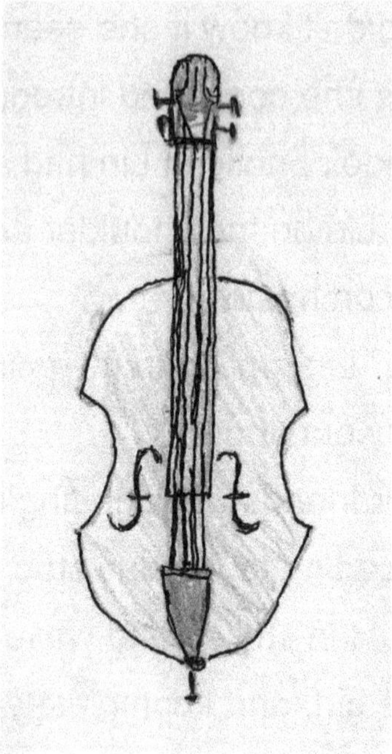

a friend like you

I watched Lin, Kani and the other three girls walk to the bus. Sometimes I wish I could go on the bus. It's like a big car pool with your classmates, but really smelly. On second thought, I'd like to stick with walking. I walked down the school courtyard and watched the September autumn leaves cartwheel across the crisp grass. The parking lot that was in between me and the high school building didn't stop me from taking that short cut. I pulled the door. Then I pushed the door.

“Locked,” I thought.

The secretary, Mrs. Wong is talking to a mom and pointing her to another office. I knocked on the glass and wrote on my whiteboard, "IT'S KELSEY!" in big letters. I lifted it up over my head and she nodded and buzzed the door open. Mrs. Wong and I are friends. I would sit in her office and wait for dad to be finished with work. Today I wasn't waiting for dad. Today I was going to study hall after school with the "big kids."

I quietly snuck in and sat at my dad's desk. All of the students were wearing Science Olympiad shirts. They all took turns to look at me with puzzled looks on their faces that said "What in the world might a middle schooler be doing here?" Only one girl out of the whole bunch had a wide grin that welcomed me to the study session.

"Embarrassing Alert!" Dad turned and looked right at me and back to the class gesturing towards me, "Class, this is my daughter Kelsey." Everyone waved and said, "Hello Kelsey" in unison.

Dad continued, "Today we'll be brushing up on our anatomy studies for Science Olympiad." That was fine, but he made it worse by saying "My daughter Kelsey's larnyx is disabled. She is unable to speak. Perhap some of you can take guesses as to why."

“Dad!” I screamed in my head. I slammed my forehead onto the desk in front of me. Ow, that hurt.

“Are you okay, dear?” Dad asked.

“Don’t call me ‘dear’ in front of the big kids Dad.” I thought. I put my thumb up. Dad was relieved.

I started my homework. In the background I hear a girl’s voice, “Blah blah anatomy. Blah blah larnyx. Blah blah other stuff.” Hmm. That’s all I heard. I finish my homework just as the class ends. Everyone leaves except for that one girl who is all smiles.

I wonder if her mouth ever gets tired from smiling?

“Great lesson today Mr. O’Brian?” is she mocking him?

“Thank you Ashlynn. Now let’s go over to my house.” dad responds.

“Ugh, Mr. O’Brian sounds so official.” I thought to myself. I like dad better. Wait. This girl is coming to my house? What for? We walked out the door and down the block. I write as Ashlynn and dad talk. When I finish my message I handed the whiteboard to Ashlynn.

She replies to my notes, “I’m going to have a lesson with your mother.”

The Voice

Lessons? With mom? Mom only taught singing. Did Ashlynn mean she taking voice lessons from mom? How many students was mom having today? When was I going to play cello in the studio?

Ashlynn went to the basement where the studio was and mom gave her lessons. I was halfway upstairs when I heard Ashlynn belt out Adele's "Someone Like You". Ashlynn's voice was that "*voice*". I know it sounds dramatic and all, but it really was. It was that "voice". If I had any voice I would want it to sound like that voice, Ashlynn's voice.

I sat on the stairs and cried. Dad looked out from his office and sat down next to me on the stairs and squeezed me using his best sympathy. He helped me up and guided me to his office. We sat together on the old couch and he read out loud our favorite book, The Giver. That helped. Then I work on my homework with earplugs so I didn't hear that voice and closed the door.

When we said our goodbyes to Ashlynn she crouched down and said words that had touched me and forever lingered. "Somewhere inside you, there's a voice wanting to come out."

Bully Who

Another awesome day at school. But the awesomeness was going to come to a complete halt at recess. Tyler was playing basketball, Zona was drawing pictures in the dirt, Yumiko and I were sitting in our favorite place under the big oak tree. Brina and her girlfriends were... flirting with boys!? Ugh, gross.

Yumiko and I talked about when we should get together and hangout. I always have to correct dad that it is a hangout, not a playdate. We outgrew playdates a long time ago. When I say "we talked," you all know by now my talking is with the whiteboard. Brina, Ida and

Cosette sauntered towards us. “What did they want?” I wrote so Yumiko could see.

“So Ida, I think Kelsey is exactly like a baby, right?” Brina said loudly so all could hear.

“You’re right again, Bri.” Ida, Brina's second-in-command girl, responds.

Cossette joins in, “Can’t talk. Never could.” They all laugh. Brina is the leader. She stops laughing and they all immediately stop as well.

“So retard, I bet you cry like a baby all day.” Brina growled.

I backed away not feeling scared but rather shocked. Mom taught me never to even think about that word. It was vulgar. Retard. It gave me the shivers. Obviously Yumiko’s mom taught her the same thing because Yumiko grasped my hand and said, “Let’s get out of here, Kelsey.” I nodded. I saw that Ida and Cossette were shocked as well.

Brina looked at those two girls and said, “Are you guys babies like Kelsey?” They shook their heads not wanting to lose their popularity and favor with Brina. Kani, on the other hand, wasn’t so concern about what Brina thought of her. She notice Brina making trouble and decided to step in.

"Listen, Brina. I'm sick of you bullying other kids, especially others who are so called *different*. You better knock it off before no one will like you anymore. I know you value your status here, but you are on popularity thin ice." Brina turned pale and stalked off. Kani winked at me and the whistle to end recess blew before I could write, "Thank You."

A cellist life

I was in the hall after school with other kids who wanted to be in concert orchestra. I found myself twiddling my hair or chewing on my nails as I waited for my turn. My name was called. I'm up. Take a deep breath, Kelsey.

I step into the small practice room and unpack my cello. In front of me was a small desk with tons of paper, music scores all over it. Behind all those papers was Mrs. Henri, the conductor. She smiled at me and said, "Hi,

Kelsey. Glad you are here. If you didn't know, my name is Mrs. Henri, your conductor."

Of course, I knew. I nodded a hello back to her.

"I see on the list you are a special needs student. Is that correct?"

Special needs? I hate that label. Well, you get what you get and you don't get upset. Forgot exactly where I got that mantra, but it works for now. I took out my whiteboard and responded, "Yes, I do not have use of my voal chords. I am mute." Another label I did not like.

Mrs. Henri didn't bat an eye. "Do you have the list of pieces you can play?" I handed what I had to Mrs. Henri. "*The Musette from English Suite Number Three* is a fine piece. Please play that one for me."

I get my bowhold in position and right before my bow touched the string, Mrs. Henri interrupts, "Don't you need your music?"

I shook my head no. I know most of my music by heart.

"Very well then, go on." Mrs. Henri scratched a few words on her note pad.

I picked up my bow again, placing it gently on the cello string. This song always moved me so I was thrilled to do it. My eyes would shut gently as the turns of the song moved down it's road. When I was at it's end there was a brief pause. I opened my eyes and looked at Mrs. Henri. She had a big smile and looked right at me. Then she applauded.

"Well done, Kelsey. It must have taken some amazing brain power to memorize a piece like that." It really doesn't take a lot for me to memorize a piece, but I smiled back at her anyway and acknowledged her compliment. I then packed my cello and waved goodbye. That response gave me a lot of confidence that I am in. I walked home with my head held high.

Later that night when I was in the family studio I played my cello again. It felt like I was singing and the cello was my vocal chords. *The Hunter Chorus* was one of my favorite songs. Gavin, my dog pranced down the stairs to listen to my music (or at least keep me company). I think Gavin enjoys the finer things in life. He would sit next to me just to listen. Mom comes down to tell me she got a call from school.

"Kelsey, you're in orchestra!"

"Hmm. Special need indeed." I thought.

Psalm 66:1

Aiden comes out of his room in his pajamas, eyes half open and feet dragging on the floor.

"Mom, I'm ready for church." He says with his eyes closed.

I snap my fingers three times in front of his face and elbow him at his side. I wish I could scream "Wake up!!" but instead I pull open his eye lids and that got him going. Aiden runs back to his room and five minutes later he says, "I'm ready now!"

Me, I got myself ready early. I'm wearing my ruffley shirt and knee length skirt, my favorite Sunday best. Aiden is wearing his purple polo shirt I got him for

Christmas and khaki shorts. I smell his breath and point to the bathroom sink. I start to walk back to my room where my favorite cream colored rose headband was until…

"Mom! Kelsey dropped a stink bomb in the bathroom!" Aiden runs down the hall pinching his nose. I turn around quickly sign in ASL, "Be quiet! You're the one who dropped that stink bomb!"

After mom finally picks a pair of shoes, we all pile into our car. I see Danika and Gavril with their mom and dad at the entrance as we drive by. Mom waves and parks and we all hop out of the car.

As the parents start gabbing about adult stuff for what seems like forever, Aiden and Gavril talk about the new lego spaceship that Aiden just bought and that I, ahem, completely assembled for him.

Danika says to me, "Nice purse." I signed "thank you" to her hoping she understands.

"Thank you, right?" she responds. I nod.

"I learned some in summer school." Danika tells me. We go sit together at church as worship singing begins. Danika dragged me to the front row so we can see the praise team. Now this is different from the old, slow and what Aiden calls boring hymns. I actually don't mind old hymns myself. But this music is different. It is peppy music you want to dance to. In some of the songs there were motions to go along with it, like sign language but more primitive or simple. After the music I thought I was going to have to sit through a long sermon but instead I went to youth group service.

The Bible passage looked at was Psalm 66:1 -- Make a joyful noise all you people. As soon as I looked at that verse I thought I couldn't worship anymore. I can't praise God with my voice. I have no voice!

The last part of the meeting we partner up and took prayer requests. Danika and I were partners. She asked me to pray for her grandmother who was in the hospital. I asked her to pray for me to have a voice. A voice to sing. A voice to praise.

Joining Together

After the school bell rang at the end of the day I saw Yumiko and a few girls walking down the hall. They were all holding volleyball practice uniforms, knee pads and gyms shoes in their hands. I tuck my music folder under my arms so I could run and catch up to them. Yumiko looks over her shoulder and stops the group.

"Hey guys, this is Kelsey." Yumiko says with a smile. They look and smile with a friendly hello. I wave back and smile also.

“Kelsey this is Kim, Thalia, Acacia, Janice and Trish.” I hope I can remember all those names. “We’re all on the volleyball team.” I give a thumbs up and point to the instrument room and wave goodbye to my good friend and her teammates.

As I step into the instrument room, many kids are buzzing around finding their instruments and getting into their places. I look and notice that the instruments are sorted in alphabetical order by which kid will be using it. I look for the “O” and find “O’Brian.” That’s mine. I pick up my case and head out a door and go to the music room. A lot of kids were already there. As I scoped out the place I saw Lin sitting at a small desk with name tags and an ipad.

Lin looked up, “Oh, hello! Glad you made it. Tap your name on the iPad for attendance and write your name on one of the name tags.” I give an “okay” sign and find my name, check it off and write my name on a name tag. I search for my seat and look up at the whiteboard. It says, “Welcome musicians!” under it is a big seating chart. I find that I have been assigned to the third row and find my seat it seems to have a stickie on it with my name. A tall African American girl stops to take that seat next to me and looks at my name tag.

“Hi Kelsey. I’m Jessica.” She waits for a response. I forgot my whiteboard! After a moment of panic I wave hello. Jessica then starts to sort her sheet music again. I tap her on the shoulder and as she turns to look at me. I touch my lips, lift my fingers off them, shake my head and make a cutting motion on my throat. She looks puzzled for a moment then guesses.

“No voice?”

I nod and smile.

“I’m sorry about that,” she responds.

I give her a thumbs up as our teacher gets the practice started. We play plenty of music that I’ve never heard before that practice. It was a blast! Next time I’m sure to bring my whiteboard.

Heart Strung

Yumiko and I sit down at our usual place for lunch. Yumiko waves an looks behind me. A small group comes to our table. I recognize them from various classes.

"Hi guys," Yumiko greets them. "How's the band coming along?"

"Oh, just fine. We are looking for a cellist still now that Lauren moved away." Kani responds.

"Kelsey plays cello, Kani. I'm sure she would be interested." I wonder if mom would approve of me joining some crazy, in her words, garage band? She is particular about music. Would dad be okay with it. And me? Do I want to do something like this? I don't know. Then I think of what my dad always said in one of his wisdom words, as he would call them. *If life gives you an opportunity, then you give the opportunity our number.* He had a lot of these I called Dadisms. So I write down our number and my email on a piece of paper that says, "Call my parents and send me an email."

Kani says, "I'll call and send that email right after school today. Here is what you should know about our band. We are called "Heart Strung." There are seven people in the band so far. You would be eight. We practice in my garage." Then everyone introduced themselves.

"Hi. I'm Maeve. I play violin."

"Hello. I'm Lin. I think we know each other already."

"S'up. I'm Perry. I play guitar for the band."

I also met Monica the artsy pianist, smart Ashton the drummer, and Wilson -- or Will -- the bass player who was very silly. Now Yumiko and I were not alone anymore. We started telling our stories; Kani told me of her life in Hawaii before moving here, that they did church outside when the weather was nice and it was always nice; Monica told me about the markets in Paris, France; and Lin told of the exotic Chinatown in California. I realized that these new friends were so welcoming, whether I had a voice or not. And into their band!

After school I plopped down my backpack and opened the snack cupboard.- Cheeze-its for today. Mom walks in.

"Hello Kelsey, how was your day?" Yea that's how all moms greet kids after school.

"Just fine, Mom," I sign. Then the phone rings. Aiden rushes down and picks up the phone, says "hello" and a few "uh huh's".

"It's for you mom," he shouts. As Aiden hands mom the phone, I glance at the caller ID. It was Kani's last name on it! I sat at the kitchen table and pulled out my Algebra review packet pretending to do homework but actually trying to hear the conversation and watch my mom's reaction. Mom decided to put it on speaker phone so I could hear.

Mom: Hello..

Kani: Please call me Kani. I am a friend of Kelsey.

Mom: Hi Kani . What can I do for you?

Kani: I would like to ask if Kelsey could join our band.

Mom: Please tell me more about this band of yours.

Kani goes on to explain about the band and the members.

Mom: Sounds Great! Feel welcome to practice in our music studio on Thursday if you need a place. Kelsey will text you our address and anything else you may need.

Kani: Thanks Mrs. O'Brian. I'm sure Kelsey will be a great addition to our band.

Mom: I am sure she will. Thank you for asking her to join. Goodbye.

Mom turns to me and says, "Go ahead and text Kani after you finish your homework. Kelsey, it sounds great." I finish my homework in no time and pick up my phone to text Kani. "Alright! I'm in!"

Too Noisy!

I stand facing the brickwall outside the artroom. Next to me was Monica, Yumiko, Tyler, Ashton and Will. I thought it was quite ironic that we had an art teacher named Mrs. Krapht (pronounced like craft). We had simple instructions to cover the wall with white paint and then come and see her when you are done. We grabbed several cans of outdoor white paint, rollers, brushes, spray paint and big sponges. There is a pause at first. Each one of us stands there and stares at the wall with a glazed look. The wall was big!

Ashton is the first to move. He picks up a spray paint can and starts to shake it up. “It’s now or never guys, come on!” We all get to work inspired by his words or at least awakened out of our glazed hypnotic state. With the entire art class working together it takes twenty minutes of our lunch time. We bring everything inside and hang up our smocks.

“Good work, kids.” Mrs Krapht exclaims. “I’ll pull you out again tomorrow for the next phase.” We grab our lunches and jackets and head over to the lunchroom. As we get to the cafeteria I see Monica cringe. It is loud. The loudest thing my ears have experienced.

“You want to eat at the office?” Will asks.

“What?” Yumiko shouts.

“YOU WANNA EAT AT THE OFFICE!”

“WHAT?”

“YOU WANNA EAT....oh never mind”

“WHAT?”

“SHHHHH.”

“Oh.”

We all walk in bracing ourselves as the decimal meter had to be at ten or above. Monica points out a food fight starting between boys and girls. Ashton steers me aside to avoid a spoonful of mash potatoes flying by.

Monica and Yumiko dodge some salad thrown by their heads.

I write, "LET'S GET A MOVE ON!" And wave my whiteboard so they all can see. They all nod. I wipe off a splash of ketchup that splattered on my board.

"You got gravy on my new designer blouse!" oh that was Brina and she was mad. "Who knows how I am going to get that stain off for goodness sake."

Sheesh. I roll my eyes. Lunch monitors try to stop the chaos, but are out numbered by middle schoolers. Lin rushes up to us with a frantic look on her face.

"I got a place." And she guides us to one of the very few calm spots in the lunchroom. As we eat we talk about how this all started. Some resemblance of order takes place as the monitors take some kids to the principal. We finished lunch and were ready to go out for a break when a monitor stops us.

"You can't go outside because of the atrocious noise you were making. Plus the terrible rucous you started." We wanted to defend ourselves but he would have none of it. Today everyone stays seated on the benches until next class begins."

In unison there is a groan and grudgingly we all sit down and wait. At least it is quiet. A little too quiet. Look at us. We are quite a sight. Will, Ashton, Tyler, Yumiko. Monica and I all in a row with the same frown and frustrated look on our face. Brina and her friends giggle.

"Quiet!" the monitor yells. It is not fair. We didn't do anything. And I didn't make a peep. I didn't make a sound. I couldn't even if I wanted to. It feels like it is going to be one long day. All I can do is put my chin on my hands and shake my head.

SPNAT

After school was out Yumiko told me to text her when I got home to see if we could study together for the quarterly math exam. I nodded and waved goodbye. I unlock my bike from the bike rack and race Aiden home. Once again I won with my special shortcut he doesn't know about.

Aiden whines, "When will you teach me your special short cut?"

"In a couple weeks on your birthday." I sign back to him.

"Yes." He mutters under his breath. "I'm going to beat you then!"

I run inside and find my mom. I slip my whiteboard under her nose with a prewritten message that says, "Mom, can Yumiko come over so we can study for the math exam?"

"Sorry sweetheart. Not today. You have S-P-N-A-T."

I sign back, "Do I have to go?"

"Yes, you have to go. I signed you up for the next four months." S-P-N-A-T stands for special need assistive team. Aiden slides into the room while I pack my bag with all the stuff I need.

"Going to splat?" he asks. I sign the letters S-P-N-A-T, not splat. I write "acronym."

"Whatever" Aiden mumbles

Mom drives me to the community center and drops me off at the front door. I've been going here the last two months. I wave at Mrs. Mendelyn who works at the front desk. I climb upstairs and open the door to Activity Room B. Ms. Lori welcomes me. She is the director of the meetings. Mrs. Helen is our translator. Today only Hannah, Drake, Rachel and Tommy were there. Hannah was deaf, Drake was blind, Rachel was in a wheelchair and Tommy had Cerebal Palsy. I sat down next to Hannah and signed “hello.”

“Hi K!” Hannah signed back.

Drake started talking about his week. That’s what we do in these meetings. Talk about what difficulties we had that week. “This week I tripped and fell because the sidewalk was filled with cracks and my walking cane got stuck in a stupid pothole or something.”

Rachel goes next. “This week I went to the bathroom and the assessible stall had bars that were too far from the toilet. It was embarrassing because I had to get help from the nurse.”

The rest of us shared our little ‘incidents’, and then we worked together to draft a letter to the principal telling of our concerns. After editing and sticking the letter in an envelope, I think we all felt better about our differences.

We meet again

I open the door to Aiden's room. He is holding Batman and Mr. Freeze Lego characters. "We meet again Batman." Aiden says I his best Mr. Freeze voice. Then he turns to me, "Hey! You were spying."

I sign back, "No. Just wanted to let you know that my friends are coming over and you are not to bother us."

"Fine," Aiden groans.

They should be here any minute now. As if on cue the doorbell rings. I run down the stairs hoping it is Kani. It is. Mom is talking to her saying something like "Hour practice, seven people, yada yada yada." Then Kani looks up at me.

"Hi Kelsey!" Her silky voice travels up the stairs to greet me. She talks as good as she sings, smooth. I smile then continue down to the basement and Kani follows me.

"Wow." She takes a big breath.

I grab my whiteboard off the piano and write, "What's in the bag?" and show the board to her.

"My bag? Oh, just my okay microphone and some sheet music." Kani pulls out a black folder with silver marker writing on it that says, "Kelsey" and the logo of the band. The logo is a heart with four strings across it with two f-shape holes it looks just like an instument from the violin family. On the back of the bag is a picture of a cello and the words "Cellist".

"Monica made them herself." Kani explains. I got goose bumps seeing it. One by one the musicians enter the studio. We all tune up and Kani starts us up.

"Okay guys, let's start with… hmmm. 'A Thousand Years' by Christina Perri."

We all shuffle through our music and pull it out. We play it together once and then figure out how it can sound mixing up the instruments.

Monica speaks up. “I want to have a piano intro first then at the closing measures I should have a lead.” I wasn’t so sure about that.

Lin added, “I think the last chorus should have just Kani and the orchestra strings.” No, I think that would be too overwhelming.

Ashton studies his music and chimes in. “Can I see the score, Kani?” Wait. Too much jumping around for me.

Kani hands him the score. “Sure. What are you thinking?”

Ashton flips a few pages of the score. “I think that the drums should be louder at the song’s climax.”

I had a hard time keeping up with the interaction everyone generated. I wanted to scream and tell everyone what I think and have them listen to me, but I just cant. In a hour everyone said their goodbyes, packed up, and thanked my mom again for the use of her studio. I tell mom I’m going to bed early. Rehearsal was exhausting.

Made with Artificial Ingredients

Sometimes I feel...fake, artificial, counterfeit, fabricated, mock, bogus and phony all wrapped in one. These words swirl in my head every single day. A girl with no voice. Psh! Who has ever heard of that? Ex-cuse me! I have. I am that girl!

Today Ashlynn comes over to help me with some homework. I am not in the greatest mood when I meet her, but she helps turn it around. She is good that way. I tell her about the band and my first practice with them.

“You are in the band with Ashton?” she says with a puzzled look on her face.

I type “yes” on my laptop since it is handy and my whiteboard is downstairs. “So what? No big deal.”

Ashlynn responds, “Uh. Yes. A huge big deal!. Ashton is my brother.” My hands float above the keyboard not knowing what to write next. I slap my hands on the keyboard “fgyguqiobó vop}?x/;” appears on the screen.

“I think that means ‘What?’” Ashlynn says as she looks at the laptop.

I nod. Ashlynn starts blabbing on about how noisy Ashton plays his drums and inconviently starts practicing when she is studying. I think she is starting to sweat as she goes on and on.

I tap her on her shoulder. She is babbling about her parents obsession with Ash trees when they named her older brother Asher, then her, Ashton, and finally her younger twin brother and sister Ashley and Ashburn. I tap her on her shoulder again as she seems to be in a trance because of all this. She looks at me and raises her eyebrows “Yes!” I pound my fist on the table and point to my ultra fat Math textbook. She and I get back to business at hand.

After some time in working on ratio and proportions we switch to my English class. I then realize I left my book, Call Of The Wild by Jack London, I was going to do a report on at school. I go over to my dad's office to ask if I can borrow his copy.

"Kelsey come here and look at this." My dad waves to have me look at something on his desk.

"All I see is Ashlynn's plastic straw ferris wheel science project" I sign to him. He gestures for me to sit next to him. I take a look at the computer on his desk.

"This is the Electro larynx." Dad begins to explain. "It is a machinery that projects the vibrations your larynx makes.

"Voice?" My eyes sparkle as he sees my signing.

Dad assures me "Artificial but yes, a voice. Let's see what the doctors think about this for you. Okay?"

I nod and hug him then walk back to see Ashlynn. A fake voice is better than no voice, I think to myself.

Bittersweet

"Guys, there's good news and bad news." Kani announces. "Bad news is Melissa Anakin got the singing solo for the talent show, not me." Looks of disappointment waves across the faces of all the band members. "Good news is that Mrs. Finch said our band can have an act since she replaced my solo with Melissa's." Shouts and whistles are heard throughout the lunchroom. We all do our secret handshake with one another.

“Let’s finish up our lunches and go to one of the practice rooms.” I practically inhale my grilled cheese sandwich and bring my Pringles on the go.

“Mrs. Henri told me we are allowed to use the school’s electric equipments for our act.” Will tells us in a voice about one octave above normal.

“Can’t wait to break in the electric viola!” Lin bounces on her toes up and down in frantic anticipation.

“I’ve heard the lights don’t work in the room where they store the equipment. Perry warns us. “We are going to need this.” He pulls out from his pocket a key chain flashlight,

“What else do you have in there?” laughs Lin. Perry digs out 75 cents, one piece of gum, a baseball card, a portable guitar tuner, and his sister’s sparkly bobbypin. All of that in his tight jean pant’s pocket. I draw a pair of cargo pants on my whiteboard and write down “you might want one of these” and show it to Perry. I get a good laugh out of him. We head to the equipment room and see a small closet door hidden behind the Timpani drum. Ashton wheels away the drum. I go to the door and twist the door knob.

Locked.

Kani snatches a key with a gold ribbon tied on it from Will and places it in my hand. “You may do the honors, Kelsey.”

I put the key in the door and turn the knob to the left. We hear a click of the lock open and so does the door. Perry was right, no lights. It could not see a thing in that room. As we all get in the door swing shut behind us. Sounds like a bad horror movie but it really happened! Monica starts freaking out. Lin reassures her that it’s okay because we still have the key.

Perry turns on his little flashlight and points it to what lies ahead. Lin, our brave band member goes ahead of us and picks up the electric viola, waving it over her head.

“Wow!” Lin whispers. She sees a small plaque attached to a stand and tells us to come look. On the plaque the writing says, “Donated by the Erikson Family.” Cool, I think to myself.

Lin plucks a string but instead of the beautiful sound of a viola, all she gets is a wirely twang noise. “Ewww!” Lin grimmaces. “This thang’s out of tune big time alright.” somtimes Lin talks like she’s from Texas or something.

We all grab the appropriate instrument and equipment we can use. Then we walk back to the door. Before I stick the key into the door, Perry says, “Wait. We need some extra amps. We can get some big sound with some add ons.”

Will says, “Alright. About four would be what we need. The practice room has one and the music room has two. That means we need to grab one out of this storage.”

Ashton was the only one of us that had his hands free so he volunteered to go back and get the extra amp. As he goes in, Monica calls out to him, “Can you also grab a pedal board for my keyboard please?”

“Yea and one for my guitar,” Perry chimes in.

“I need one as well,” says Maeve and Will.

So as we walk out of the room Ashton ends up with so much stuff we can barely see his head sticking out of all the equipment he is carrying. We get to the practice room and set up quickly.

"Back to ‘Thousand Years’ guys,” Kani announces.

After we play through for the first time Maeve jumps in, “I think I should play the intro with Monica.”

“I like the intro to be a solitary piece.” Monica shoots back.

“It sounds too plain.”

“Are you criticizing my playing.”

“No. It just it needs....”

"Stop!" Kani tries to cut in.

"You are not in this, Kani." Maeve responds in annoyance. "Leave this between Monica and me." All of a sudden everyone is in this petty fight about the intro, which is not about the intro. No one is looking to what I think. I decide to stand up and walk towards the door.

"Kelsey, wait!" I guess Ashton noticed me as he raised his voice above everyone else's. But I just walk out and slam the door behind me. The noise of bickering stops suddenly and all there is is silence.

Voice specialist

Bing! The elevator reaches the third floor. My dad and I step out and walk down the corridor. We enter room 306. It smells of disinfectant and medicine. Eww. There is a reception desk with a nurse sitting behind it.

"Hello!" she chirps with a cheery smile like those annoying Robins at 5 o'clock in the morning. "What can I do for you today?"

"We are here to see Dr. Megan Oslo," answers dad.

"Voice therapy is in room 9. Please take a seat." Dad and I sit down.

"Ready?" Dad asks. I nod and gulp.

"Kelsey?" A nurse speaks as she pops into the waiting room. My dad and I stand up and follow the nurse. "Dr. Olso is waiting for you." The nurse opens the door for us.

"Hello, Doctor Olso. Please to meet you," Dad is quick to say.

"Nice to meet you. Please, everyone calls me Dr. Megan."

I do the only logical thing that comes to mind and sign, "Hi. My name is Kelsey." Dr. Megan watches my hands carefully.

"Nice to meet you, Kelsey." Dr. Megan replies. She continues talking to us about how a good quality electro larynx can be so useful for me. She explains the cost, coverage by insurance and the process of therapy to train for using it. Dad is very ivolved, me not so much. I get to see a picture of the exact model. *The Blom Singer EL1000 perfect for voice handicaps use everyday.* Dr. Megan shows us a video of a girl using it. She doesn't even sound like a girl! Not even a person! She sounds like a robot! I start to rethink this electro thingie mabobber. We look over a handout with the goals for therapy and the length of time to get use to it.

"I am very optimistic that this will greatly improve your life Kelsey." Dr Megan assures me.

As soon as we get home I hastily log in to my laptop and suddenly have a burst of excitement I sign "Hurry up Dad. Come on. We need to order one of these now!"

A voice first heard

After numerous training drills, reaching goals and endless trips to the therapy office, the day has finally arrived. It started with me placing the electrolarynx on my throat.

“What goal am I working on today, Dad?” a robotic noise came out of the amp.

“You’ve accomplished all of them already.” He replies.

“Really?”

"Yes, Kelsey, all of them."

That day Dad stuck it in my backpack without me knowing. When I got to my locker, I felt it in my backpack. Pulling the electrolarynx out, I just stared at it. The Blom-Singer Electrolarynx EL1000. I remember being so excited the day I received it. Since then I have had a lot of mix feelings.

A younger student in the hall saw me with it and asked, "Is that a flashlight? What do you need a flashlight for in school?" I could have demonstrated it to him with a voice answer, but I instead just pretended I didn't hear him. The bell rang and I shove it into the depths of my backpack and pull out my whiteboard to be ready for anymore social interactions.

Ten days pass by and Mr. Electro-larynx still in the deep darkness of my backpack, never seeing the light of day. Finally I bring it out at Ms. Kris's classroom and show it to her.

"Cool, Kelsey. Would love to hear you use it." Not today.

Ten more days pass. This time I take a deep breath and pack it in my pencil case where it would be easily assessable. I see Ms. Kris in the hallway and show her the machine as my hands are shaking as I hold it out.

It is like holding a thick six-inch stick. It has blue lettering on top of a silvery grey backing with a mike like top.

Ms. Kris smiles. “I’ll come with you to class.” I file into the classroom with all the other kids. Very casually I sat. At least I thought in my mind but I was sweating inside big time. Ms. Kris went to talk to Mrs. Adams, my English teacher. Ms. Kris then prepares the class by telling them about the Electro-larynx and how it works.

“Class, the Electro-larynx is a device used to project the voice of the person using it. It picks up the vibration of…”

I had heard this a million times before. Hopefully they would be ready for the strange noise that would come out of me. The class begins with everyone giving a short summary of the book they read. It was Yumiko’s turn. She told the class of Divergent. (our favorite book)

Then I was up. I stood up and looked at Ms. Kris. She gave a thumbs up this time with her wide grin. I pulled my electro-larynx up to my throat and started my summary of Call of the Wild. After I finished I heard a few muddled laughs and giggles. I slouched in my seat and hid behind my book. Did I mention the machine makes me sound like a robot?

Then after a moment of silence a burst of applause cried out throughout the classroom. For me?! My face transformed, a smile all the way across from ear to ear and a small dose of wetness in my eyes.

I walked home relieved and hopeful. When I got inside I looked for an apple. Yes! A honeycrisp apple, the apple that is on the top of my favorite all time apples. Then I went to the pantry for some peanut butter. All gone. I suspect Aiden got the last of it. Took a napkin to take with my apple and headed to my room. As I walked down the hallway, I peeked into Aiden's room. He was talking to Fuzzie. Aiden hears the door creak open.

"Watch out Fuzzie! It's the enemy spy, Kelsey!" Fuzzy and Aiden are wearing sunglasses and are covered in peanut butter. I rolled my eyes and go to my room. I have been awarded a no homework pass today so I grab luvie.

"Where's the peanut butter?" Luvie exclaims.

"Fuzzie with all his fuzziness got it all stuck in his fur. Now it's all matted down." I explain to Luvie. "Mom is not going to be happy."

"Yeah." Luvie responds. "They are in trouble!" I pulled out my tiny plastic brush from my old Barbie suitcase and brush Luvie's soft downy fur.

"It was a good day today at school Luvie." I tell her.

"Really? Tell me what happen."

Grandma says Aiden and I are too old to be talking to stuffed animals. I think the older I am the more I need Luvie to talk to.

The Sound of Music

It's FroYo Friday! We all jump in the car and drive to Yogurtland. When we get there Aiden knows exactly what he wants. Aiden grabs a cup and helps himself to the Nutella flavor yogurt and piles on the Gummi Bears and kiwi. Weird and gross but least he adds fruit to all that candy.

I decide to try something new. I see a flavor call Taro. Hmm. I remember Yumiko talking about Taro on cultural heritage day. Taro is a sweetened purple yam. I sample it just to make sure. Yum! I swirl myself some into my cup. I add blueberries and mochi balls, which are little mushed up rice balls. I love mochi. It's chewy, pasty with a light sweetness to it. Aiden like to stretch it. I guess my description of it doesn't do it justice. Trust me it's great.

Dad gets his usual dark chocolate with peanut butter clusters. Aiden and I inherited his peanut butter addiction. He almost gets away with no fruit until mom spies his cup and dumps some bananas into it. Mom's rule: Must Have Fruit. Mom gets her usual mango smoothie. We sit down at a table.

"I heard there is the *Sound of Music* playing at the old Harvey's theatre. Harvey always sets up old plays. My dad loves it. I think hard about it. I like the idea but it is not the same as listening to live singers for a couple hours. Aiden as no hesitation as he bursts out with excitement.

"I want to go! I love that movie." You usually don't see a boy his age get excited about an old musical. Aiden is not a usual boy. Mom explains that it is not a movie, but a play. We would see a live performance. I like that idea.

I sign, "Yes." I left my electro-larynx at home, not liking to use it in public yet.

“Okay. It’s settled. We go tomorrow.” Dad announces.

The next morning Aiden invites me to sit in the laundry room with him and wait for Fuzzie and Luvie to come out from the wash. As soon as we hear the beeping noise of the dryer we excitedly swing open the door and tear into all the clothes, like we would opening presents on Christmas morning. Aiden is halfway into the dryer seeking Fuzzie. He throws Luvie behind him right into my face. Luvie smells great. Then goes Dad’s underwear, Mom’s blouse, Aiden’s socks, and my shorts. I dump all of them into the laundry basket under my feet. At the very back of the dryer was Fuzzie, looking a bit dizzy but clean as could be. Soon all the laundry was put away, and Aiden and I could bask in the fragrance of our clean stuffed animals.

Later that day we were having dinner. It is Chinese food this night. I am slurping down my noodles from my Won Ton Mein soup and dad tells us, “The show starts at 6:30. So we will have to leave right after we put the dishes in the dishwasher.”

We drive to the theatre in fifteen minutes. Not a minute to spare, we get our tickets and I get a small bag of popcorn for Aiden and myself. We walk into the auditorium and find our seats as the orchestra is warming up. Love hearing the instruments making a bundle and bash of sounds. As the show begins, I am captivated by the actors' singing abilities. Singing puts words and emotions all into one package.

"That was awesome!" Aiden exclaims. Most of his friends would only say that about transformers and ninja turtles but not Aiden. I give him a double five.

When we get home I help dad with his grading papers. He lets me put stickers on the tests. I put smiles and hearts and other goofy images. I place one on Ashlynn that says "You are a star!" and I giggle to myself thinking about what her reaction will be.

Dad says to me, "I have something to give you Kelsey." I thought it would be one of his goofy stickers and place it on my forehead. I got myself prepared. Instead he hands me a DVD. So I place it into the side slot of his computer and there is some music from a guy I never heard of before. His name is Peter Frampton. He is a skinny guy with long hair playing his guitar and singing to a mike on a stand. Dad says he was popular when he was my age. Whew. Ancient music. I smile.

In the middle of the song I hear a sound that goes "Wah wah wah" and he is putting his mouth to a plastic tube that runs down the mike and is connected to his amp. The audience is going crazy over the sound he makes through this, what my dad told me later was his "Wah Wah" pedal. Go figure.

I point to my electrolarynx, look at my dad and he smiles and nods.

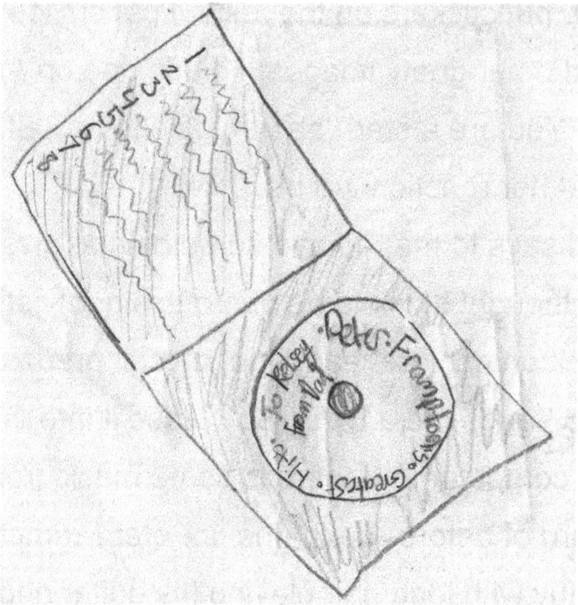

Yu and Mi

I stuff my watermelon pajamas in my duffle bag and cover up Luvie with my sleeping bag. I carefully place my electrolarynx on top of everything and zip up the bag. Walking down the stairs I see my dad and give him a thumbs up.

"Ready to go K?"

"All ready Dad."

Aiden and Mom are waiting in the car as dad take my bag and puts it in the trunk. We drive over to the south side of town where Yumiko's family live. When we get there, Aiden rushes to the door so he can ring the bell. Always wanting to ring doorbells.

"Ding dong." Yumiko's mother opens the door. My mom holds out her hand.

"You must be Hatsuko." Yumiko's mother shakes my moms hand.

"And you must be Alaina. Please come in and join us. We are so glad you can have dinner with us." We walk inside and a delicious aroma fills my nose. Mmmm, looking forward to whatever is making that smell. Yumiko is standing next to her grandma at the stove. She acknowledges me and nods for me to come and look over her shoulder to see what's cooking.

When I am standing behind her, Yumiko says, "Obachan, meet Kelsey my friend."

"Kombawa Kelsey-san."

Yumiko whispers in my ear, "She is saying hello or more specifically, good evening." I give Yumiko's Obachan a slight bow. She smiles at me and bows back. I write on my board for Yumiko to see, "Your grandma is sooo cute." Yumiko giggles.

Yumiko asks if I would like to help. I nod. I love helping out in the kitchen and giving a hand wherever I can. So she gives me a wooden spoon and has me stir the noodles so they won't stick together. Yumiko goes to the counter and chops up some green onions. Wow. She's fast. I might lose a finger if I cut like that! I continue to observe she and her Obachan at work. Obachan dips shrimp and green beans into the panko batter. It's kind of like bread crumbs but lighter. She dips it into the hot oil and lets it fry for a short while. Then she fishes it out of the oil and lays it on some paper towels. Yumiko pulls out some bowls and I put the noodles and broth into the bowls. Obachan carefully places the shrimp and green beans on top. Looks like a piece of art that you can eat!

As we are about to eat, Mrs. Kimura calls out, "Akichan come downstairs and meet our guest!"

Bouncing ever so lightly down the stairs comes a girl with baggy clothes and long ebony hair encircling her face so all you can see are her rectangular glasses and a smile. She is a bit older than us but it is hard to tell. She waves at me and I wave back.

"Kelsey this is my cousin Akira." Yumiko makes the introduction. "If you speak to her she will not answer. She is deaf."

So I smile again and nod my head to her. There is constant conversation over the table and I make a few notes to Yumiko on my whiteboard. I even draw a stick figure to have Akira see. I think she was amused. After dinner, my family get ready to go and Dad tells me to "be good".

After they are gone, Akira pulled out a box from the closet. Yumiko excitedly calls me into the kitchen and Akira follows with the box in hand. Her mom is with us and she pulls out a special bag of rice.

"We are going to make mochi, Kelsey!" Yumiko can barely contain herself. "It's the greatest desert ever."

So after washing the rice and placing it in the machine, we go and play a little bit of video games that Akira had brought from Japan. The mochi machine was making a pounding noise a little like a washer does when it has too much clothes.

"Ding!" the machine rings.

"Okay. It's done. Let's make some goodies." Her mom lays out various powders and we make these little sticky rice balls and roll it into the powder. I was told to try this tan brown powder that is a little sweet. The mochi was so chewy and stretchy. I loved it. Fun food. After trying a one more with sweet beans put inside of the mochi ball I was stuffed.

Then we went upstairs to Yumiko's room. I unpacked my pajamas and discovered that Yumiko has a matching pair. She giggled. I smiled. I lay out my Owl sleeping bag. Yumiko lays out her Panda bag.

Lastly, I pull out Luvie and Yumiko asks, "Who's that?"

I lift up my electro-larynx and introduce her to Luvie. "Oh this is just my stuffed animal, Luvie." Up until now I had not used the electro-larynx. Yumiko heard it before but I am still shy about it. She is very understanding.

I pause a moment then say, "I talk to her some times when I need to get something off my chest or just when I am feeling lonely or sad or confused or mad or happy or excited..."

Yumiko goes over to her bed and pulls out a stuffed Pokemon Snorlax. I surprise myself that I know it is a Snorlax. That comes from having a younger brother.

"I talk to mine too." She says with a smile. Lot of smiling goes on in a sleepover at Yumiko's, I guess.

When we go to bed and lights were out I thought I heard a little voice in the room.

"So Snorlax, how are those mochi balls?"

"Yummy."

"Good to know." I knew that voice.

"Goodnight, Luvie." I whispered. "Goodnight, Snorlax."

***

The next morning we have pancakes made from their rice cooker! It was extra fluffy, more like a angel food cake. Awesome! Then Yumiko showed me some beautiful ink paintings hanging on the walls in the breakfast nook. They were ones with cherry blossoms, Koi fish, and mountain sceneries.

"Beautiful." I remarked with my electro-larynx. "You drew these yourself?"

"I did." Yumiko nods and has a glow as she looks at me.

"These are amazing! I am in absolute awe." I think I made her blush a bit.

"Why, thank you, Kelsey. I am very flattered."

After I pack up all my stuff in my duffle bag, my parents stop by to pick me up. I say my goodbye's and thank you's to everyone. Obachan gives me a hug and tells me to come back soon. On the way home I tell my parents all about my sleepover. I didn't even think twice about using my electro-larynx. It has become more and more natural to use. As long as I am with people I trust.

Accepting Forgiveness

I'm playing picnic with Aiden, Luvie, Fuzzie, and Gavin. Granny says I'm too old for picnic playing. She must think I'm very old. But I'm still young at heart. Gavin starts walking all over the tea set. I give him his peanut butter Kong and he settles down right next to me.

Mom says, "Kelsey, Kani just called to ask if you were going to her house for band." I nod slowly and pack my cello. Taking my lanyard neck strap that has my house keys on it, I place it over my head and proceed out the door. Mom follows me. I dig out my Electro-larynx from my jean pockets and lift it to my throat.

"I can go by myself, Mom. Kani is only a couple blocks away."

"Okay, dear." Mom responds. "Don't forget to look both ways before crossing the street." These are the moments my mom, in contrast to Granny, reminds me of how young I am in her eyes.

At Kani's place, I go out through the garage and pressing the code number she gave me, and magically the garage door rolls opens. Perry is fiddling with Kani's adjustable microphone with his screwdriver on his Swiss army knife.

He looks at me and says, "Hey guys, Kelsey's here." Kani rushes up to me and tightly squeezes me.

"I'm so sorry!" she blubbers through a waterfall of tears. "I thought you weren't coming back. I'm so glad you are here." Maybe this is a good time to give her the handkerchief I made at sewing club. I hand it to her and she strokes the soft seagreen cloth. Kani notices at the top left corner of the handkerchief her embroidered name and a coral pink Hibiscus flower. She folds it up, gives me a hug and informs me it is too nice to put her snots on it.

"Let's get started, peeps!" she shouts so to move right into practice.

Tonight you can hear the music fill the air without any argument. We are tight and together. At the end of playing, I use my Electro-larynx and ask, "Hey, guys can we use my Electro-larynx in our next song?"

"How?" ask Will.

"Like this." I pull out the CD stereo Kani has I the corner of the garage and put in my dad's Peter Frampton music. Everyone is smiling and looks at me with a unified warmth that makes me smile back.

"All in favor say yes." Kani says to make it official.

Eight voices with one being robotic shouts, "Yes!"

The rest of the night we practiced and played with all the possibilities of me using my voice to sing.

Changes

I walk outside and realize how much has changed since that day six years ago. The sapling tree outside our house has turned into a big Elm. Yumiko riding her bike down the street, no longer having that Pixie haircut from back in junior high. I wave high to Danika who is watering her flowers and has colored part of her hair bright red. I, myself, have added some color, not in my hair but on my toes. Today it is for all to see with all ten hanging out of my flip-flops and the blue nail polish shines. A lot of my friends are outside today.

There is Aiden on our driveway in his sports shirt and basketball shorts. That would be okay if it wasn't for his bright green socks and matching shoes. He never wore clothes like that until this year. I guess we all change.

"Heading to the park to play ball with Anthony and Jaden!" he shouts across the yard. "And hurry up and get the mail so you can tell me if I got anything from Sophie!" Sophie is his new squeeze. I roll my eyes. One thing that hasn't changed is I still see him as a brat. Sometimes I just wish the past could come back and he would still be that little boy I chased out of my room all the time. I retrieve the mail and shuffle through it.

"Nothing for you, Aiden." I smile as I give him the bad news. It is bills, junk mail, a magazine for mom, and what appears to be an official letter from the Julliard School of Music addressed to me, Kelsey O'Brian. Wait. What? This must be their response to my application. I go inside and put the rest of the mail on the kitchen table. Then I take the letter to my room.

"Nice mail. What's in it?" Luvie inquires.

“Thanks. It’s from Julliard. I think it is their response to my application. This could be my future for the next four years!”

“Kelsey, will you take me to college with you?”

“Of course!” I reply.

“Yay!” Luvie says.

I open the letter. This is what is on it:

Dear Ms. Kelsey O’Brian,

We are happy to inform you that you have been accepted into Julliard School of Music…

I silently scream.

Then I call my parents upstairs and they enter into my room.

“Is it what I think it is?” Mom nervously asks.

I confirm by bouncing on my toes barely able to contain my body. My mom joins in. Even my dad starts bouncing. They both rush to me and squeal out with joy. Almost squeezed the life out of me.

“I made it.” I thought to myself and smiled.

Epilogue

I am writing a letter to Mom and Dad. I've been at college for about two months now. I put down my pen (they still rather get a handwritten note than email). I will give it a rest and come back to it later. I pulled out Luvie from under my pillow and pick her up. My roommate Annabelle is out. So I can talk freely.

"Hi Luvie."

"Hi."

"You miss, Fuzzie?"

"Uh huh."

"I miss Mom and Dad and Aiden and Gavin too." I say with a sigh.

The door creaks open and before I can put Luvie away, Annabelle walks in.

"Hey. Who are you talking to?" Might as well let her in. I hold up Luvie.

"Just talking to my stuffed animal. This is Luvie." I waited for her to tease me.

"Well it's about time!" she digs under her bed and pulls out a stuffed sheep.

"Meet Huggie."

I think the whole dorm floor heard the roars of hysteria coming out of our room coming out of our room that night. One similar to any laugh they heard their whole life. Another very unique laugh with a voice once long gone and then found and celebrated.

Facebook
Kelsey O'Brien
→ Adabelle Winston
Dorm room sleepover!
like
comment
Aiden O'Brien
Just watched a movie with Sophie at AMC Movie theater

The End

More books from the author:

An Island and a Chance, written at the age of eight

Letters from Brooklyn, written at the age of nine

Find them on Amazon.com